33
TIPS
for
WORKING REMOTELY

CARMEN CORRAL

Copyright © 2020 Carmen Corral

All rights reserved

Translator: Amber Aguilar

ISBN: 9798682949939

For everyone who believes that change is a vital constant and, above all, for everyone who refuses to accept it.

For my sister, for her unconditional support across the miles.

CONTENTS

My first time		7
The way we work is changing		9
Who this book is for		11
1.	Don't let advantages turn into disadvantages	15
2.	Think of it like training	18
3.	Find your place	20
4.	Don't blame your environment; accept and adapt	23
5.	Find others' place (and put them there)	26
6.	Get ready to start working	28
7.	Take control of your schedule	31
8.	Find out when you're most productive	34
9.	Create a routine	38
10.	Escape your routine	41
11.	Change positions	43
12.	Rest	46
13.	Set boundaries for bosses and clients	49
14.	Adapt productivity techniques to your needs	52
15.	Schedule your tasks	54
16.	Focus on what's essential	57

17. Work in blocks	59
18. Take things little by little	61
19. Don't obsess over productivity	63
20. Distract the distractions and interrupt the interruptions	65
21. Make tools your biggest ally	68
22. Don't lose yourself in tools	71
23. Communicate more clearly	75
24. Limit your number of meetings	78
25. Make the most out of videocalling	80
26. Relate to others	83
27. Understand your inseparable colleague: you	86
28. Have a weekly meeting with yourself	89
29. Plan the day before	92
30. Celebrate what you've achieved	95
31. Set an end to your working day	97
32. Switch off	99
33. Deal with inspiration properly when it comes	101
33 more tips for developing your skills	104

My first time

The first time I had the chance to work from home was a one-off from my conventional nine to five office job. I was involved in a project which required maximum concentration and had to write a report. I was working in Human Resources. If you've ever spent a couple of minutes in the HR department at your company, you'll know it's not exactly all silence and serenity.

My boss told me: "If you want, stay at home for a day and do the work there, so you don't get distracted." I took him up on it – at least, the working from home part. The "no distractions" part wasn't so simple.

I got up early, ready and raring to work from home. It was novel and exciting. But despite my motivation to be a super-productive worker-from-home, I realized it was mid-morning and I'd had two breakfasts, done a load of laundry, and organized my closet, but not actually written more than a single sentence of my report. Every time I sat down in front of my computer, I thought of something more interesting I could be doing. Even hanging out the laundry seemed more appealing.

The afternoon wasn't much better. When I finally parked myself in my chair and resolved not to get up for another hour, I compared the day's news on several sites and watched a cute cat video. Dinnertime rolled around and my report wasn't even a page long. In short, I had "worked" from 8 in the morning to 11 at night – fifteen hours – to complete a job that should have taken five or six.

That was the day I discovered that working from home isn't as easy as it sounds.

It requires some practice and training. That's the good news: you can learn to be productive while working from home – even more so than in the office.

That was back in 2007. Since then, I've had the opportunity to do remote work for several companies, for myself, from home, from coworking spaces, in cafes, on planes, buses and trains, at the beach, in the mountains, and in several time zones.

The way we work is changing

Up till now, what's mattered to companies has been having us in the office for eight hours. Now, results are more important. Some companies claim to evaluate their employees based on the goals and results they've achieved, but this isn't completely honest. They preach about only being interested in results and a job well done, yet they have entry and exit control systems and employees have to clock in. Under these conditions, are results really what matter most? More modern companies promote flexible working hours – but even then, what would happen if an employee supposed to work eight hours a day achieved results by arriving every day at 11 and leaving at 4pm? And when I say results, I'm talking about overall good work, performance, proper quantity and quality, and so on.

With remote working, except in a few cases, your company has no control over how long you sit at your desk. That makes a lot of companies and a lot of bosses feel uneasy. It makes some employees feel uneasy, too, because they wonder if they'll be fairly assessed and if their work will be valued now that no one can see how long they're sitting doing it. We all need to change our mindset: companies, bosses, and employees.

Before, going into the office every day and spending eight hours there meant you had already held up part of the deal – the other part, of course, being your actual work. Now that no one can see you sitting in front of your computer, one part of that vanishes, and all the focus is now on the work you do.

Remote work involves more changes than simply your place of work. It's not just about grabbing your laptop, taking it home, and working there. It's more complex than that. It encompasses a lot of things, and requires a process of change on numerous levels.

The pandemic has landed us all working remotely, with no idea how to do it, without the means, and without any preparation for it. The good thing is that it has brought us the great opportunity to work from home, which might otherwise have taken years or even decades to come.

Companies and people who have begun working remotely due to the quarantine have done so in the worst possible conditions. Things can only get better from here.

Remote working is here to stay. It's up to you to adapt to it and to make the most of all the benefits it offers.

Who this book is for

I decided to write this book because I have been working remotely for years, and people often ask me for advice on being more productive, how to cope with distractions, or how to get organized. But that's not my biggest motivation for writing this. To answer those questions, I could simply recommend you one of many books on personal productivity that others have written, and point out the most important tips to apply to remote working. The main reason I'm writing this book is to shine a little more light on the "personal" in "personal productivity".

Allow me to explain: most books on productivity are based around the idea that there are a few rules applicable to everything, and formulas that work for everyone. They forget that every person is their own world, and there is a world full of people.

That's why this book aims to guide you in discovering what works for you, so you can work remotely in the most effective way possible (for you), taking advantage of the flexibility remote working offers.

Another of my main motivating factors for writing this book instead of just recommending a good book on productivity is that remote working isn't just about moving from the office to your house. If it were just about that, my first time remote working would have been more fruitful. Remote working is about much more than that. It involves changing your mindset, your way of doing things, of getting organized, of relating to people, and more. We'll talk about all of this as the book goes on.

This book is for you if:

- You're starting out remote working and you need some support to help you adapt to this new way of working.

- You already work remotely and you want to take it to the next level, get more organized and be more efficient.

- You think you could still get more out of your day-to-day.

- You want to take maximum advantage of the flexibility that remote working offers.

You won't find magic formulas in this book that will allow you to start working from home – or anywhere else – overnight without even feeling it and with more productivity than ever.

It's not a book of productivity tips with detailed instructions you have to follow to a T. Nor is it full of personal productivity techniques that seem easy on paper, but are hard to put into practice and cause more issues than they resolve.

What you *will* find in this book is:

- Tips for discovering what personally works best for you when it comes to being productive while remote working.

- The differences between remote working and office working, and how to adapt to them.

- Key ways to plan and organize better while remote working.

There are many types of job that can be done remotely and in very different conditions. For example, some allow for total time flexibility, which has advantages and disadvantages we'll look at later. In other jobs, even when done remotely, you have to respect a strict timetable – usually for customer service reasons.

Some of these tips won't apply to you, whether because of your personal preferences or because of the characteristics of your job. All I ask, before you discount them, is that you're not making excuses to do so. Every time you find yourself thinking (or saying out loud – I won't call you crazy for talking while you read) the old "it's impossible to do that at my company" or the other chestnuts "chance would be a fine thing" and "sure, like it's that easy", stop for a moment, breathe, and read it again. Then, read it again – this time, without judging or applying it directly to your situation. Look at it objectively first, before deciding if it suits your needs or not, if it's possible to apply some element of it. And if it's not useful to you, don't throw it away (I don't want the pages of this book, that I wrote with so much care, to end up in the trash either literally or figuratively). Anything you now think you can't apply, file away for the future in some corner of your mind. One day, it may be useful to you, or it may inspire you to create your own version suited to your needs.

1. Don't let advantages turn into disadvantages

Remote working has a lot of advantages, the main two being: you don't have to leave your home, and you have flexible hours.

If you don't need to leave home to start working, you'll save a lot of time on travel. You'll also avoid the stress of traffic or crowded public transport. But not having to go out to get to work can present some difficulties, too.

Some people find it hard to get to work without changing their surroundings, staying in the same place where they live out their family lives. You have to get in the right "mode", and somehow let your brain know you've arrived at your place of work. It's not just the house you live in any more; it's your office, too.

The distractions you get at home are different from the ones you have at the office. As well as everything on your computer, as if that weren't enough, you also have your kitchen, stocked with food at all hours. Housework isn't exactly fun, but when you should be working, you find yourself drawn to it.

Flexible hours are another big advantage.

You'll have the freedom to start work when you want, and finish when you want. You can distribute your working hours over the course of the day however you wish, enabling you to attend to personal matters such as picking the kids up from school, running a mid-morning errand, or simply taking a break to catch up with a friend over coffee.

Don't let that flexibility become a disadvantage. Making your working day flexible can work in your favor, but if you don't control it, it will turn against you. If you don't set a time for finishing work, your day can stretch to infinity (and beyond). Feeling that you spent all day working – even if you didn't – is exhausting.

These are the two sides of the coin of these two features of remote working. There are others, and they're worth identifying, in both the advantages and disadvantages they present.

To start with, take a moment to answer the following questions:

What are the advantages of remote working for you?

What obstacles do you face remote working? Think about the external roadblocks and difficulties you will – or think you will – have to take on, such as those to do with your company and the people around you. Then, think about the internal ones that have to do with you: your beliefs and your personal resistance to remote working.

2. Think of it like training

No one is born knowing it all. Everything takes practice. Don't expect to start working remotely today and find that everything is miraculously perfect and you're the world's most productive person. You will need some time to adjust, practice and train yourself.

Think of it that way: like training.

The first day you go to the gym, you have to find out what kinds of classes and machines they have. Little by little, you discover which exercises you like doing and what routine you'll follow. You'll try a few different things, sticking with some and leaving others.

When you start working out, you don't lift 20kg the first day if you've never done it before. And if you've never worked remotely before, you'll have to take it little by little too. Be patient with yourself.

Some days will be great and you'll be giving it your all. Some, it'll seem as if you tried hard for nothing, and some you'll feel you barely had to try and you still got everything done. Don't obsess over bad days or blame yourself for then. Get ready for the next day remember that there are always good and bad days.

Acknowledge your progress, everything you've learned, and the obstacles you've overcome since starting to work remotely. Congratulate yourself and celebrate.

3. Find your place

Now that you're working remotely, it's up to you where you do it. You don't have to limit yourself to just one place. You have multiple options, from any room in your house (yep, you can work from the bathroom) to cafés and coworking spaces. Why not try several locations before deciding which you like best and where you feel most comfortable and productive? This will also depend on the type of task you're carrying out – for example, if you have hour-long phone calls to make, a café probably isn't the best idea.

Once you've tried some places, you can decide on the best one for working.

And you don't always have to do it from the same place. Variety is the spice of life for many people. Doing different tasks in different places will help your brain to associate that place with that task, and it'll be easier to get in the right mindset to focus on it.

If you're not the kind of person who likes to move around and you would rather stay in one place, choose the best one and decorate it how you like. I don't mean spending hours poring over the IKEA catalog finding the best furniture and accessories. It's much more simple than that.

Simply make it yours, little by little. Maybe you'd rather that wall-facing desk was by the window, or those books piled up on it are bothering you. Have everything you need to hand, so you don't have to get up to find things and get sidetracked.

Think about your workspace in the broadest terms. Do you like to listen to music while you work? Maybe at your office, that was looked down upon. Well, now you can. Create a work playlist: songs you like and that help you concentrate and get to work. Different musical styles put us in different moods, so some tasks are better to suited to certain styles.

Let's take it a little further. As well as your external environment, you have your inner environment. How do you feel today? Are you worried about anything? How are your energy levels? Give your inner state a check-up before you start working; you'll have to work with it, and it can impact you even more than your external surroundings.

You wouldn't start working in a room that was turned upside down, with papers everywhere – on the table, on the floor, even yesterday's old food lying round. If it's messy in your mind, not your room, it'll be even harder to get to work.

Do a quick scan of how you feel.

Acknowledging your mental state will help give you an idea of how your working day will go.

If your head is full of worries, admitting that they're there will help you leave them aside for a while so you can work and focus on other things. I know it's easier said than done, but recognizing your worries is the first step.

Take care of your external and internal environments.

4. Don't blame your environment; accept and adapt

Whether or not you've found your workspace, don't blame your surroundings for low productivity, distractions, or for how hard it is to work in those conditions.

Everyone who dreams or has once dreamed of being a writer imagines themselves writing in some idyllic, isolated place, away from the rest of the world and free from distractions. Whether sea or mountain views, we usually daydream about a desk overlooking a beautiful, tranquil paradise. Crystalline waters and waves lapping against the shore, or the quiet stillness of a mountain lake: a setting to inspire our best literary works. Works never written – because even if we're lucky enough to write in such a sublime environment, we find that inspiration and productivity don't live there, either (I speak from experience).

Our surroundings help us feel comfortable, but working efficiently is up to us. If you don't bring it, your environment will end up taking the blame for every excuse under the sun. "I can't work with the noise from the street outside", "how can I concentrate with the kids asking me for things every second?", "this chair is so uncomfortable", and so on.

Stop for a moment and think: when you were in your office, were your surroundings always ideal? Your colleague telling you about her new cookie recipe, right when you needed to get some work done (and were hungry)? Your other colleague jabbering loudly into the phone? Your department relocated to some windowless part of the office where you never see sunlight?

Changing your environment and the ecosystem around you is more difficult than simply conforming to the one you're in.

Make the most of the times your surroundings enable you to be most productive. When it comes to organizing your time, take your environment into account. Above all, if you're working from home and you have a family, there will be times more conducive to work and others where it's harder to concentrate. Bear this in mind when planning your days. Do the tasks that require more concentration when you're alone and things are quieter.

Adjust to the hours during which you find it easiest to work in the environment. For example, if you know it'll be harder for you to focus once your kids get home from school, no matter how hard you try to work through the noise, then adapt to that and work before they get back. If you don't have enough time, maybe you could get up earlier in the morning, or work for an hour after they've gone to bed. Don't throw out any of these options or any specific time period; adapt to the conditions of your surroundings.

There's a solution for everything if you try, and this isn't always an external thing.

A new workspace can sometimes present a barrier to working remotely. However, even when an obstacle seems clearly external, that may not always be the case. Often, they are mental obstacles we use as an excuse not to work remotely.

Your external environment is never going to be perfect. Never – until you accept it how it is. As long as you don't, it will simply be your excuse not to do the things you need to do. As soon as you find a solution and accept that it is possible to work in your environment just as it is, you'll find that you can work just as comfortably and efficiently (or even more so) than when you were in the office. You'll be just as productive as if you were in that idyllic place you envisaged.

5. Find others' place (and put them there)

You've found your workspace. But if you're working from home and you don't live alone, you'll probably have to share some hours with your delightful family (who may not seem so delightful from time to time).

Does this scenario resonate with you?

You pick the kids up from school, get home, give them a snack, tell them to do their homework quietly, and start working. Five minutes later, you hear: "Dad, she's being mean to me" or "Mom, I lost the book Grandpa gave me".

To avoid this happening, you need to put them in their place, both literally and figuratively. First, make it totally clear that you are not to be bothered. Be consistent and stick to your word. The second part is a little more complicated. It requires some practice and adjustment, but if you persist, you can do it. It involves ignoring them when they appear. Don't pay them any attention – don't even answer the simplest questions just to get them to go away, because if you do, they'll go away that one time and then do it again tomorrow.

Make sure they understand that when you're

working, you're not doing anything for anyone. Make it clear when you start and finish work. If you have a home office, the simplest thing is to tell them not to bother you when you're in that room or when the door is shut.

If you're working in a shared area of your home, you could use headphones – both to block out noise and to send the signal that you are not to be bothered. It works! But you have to train them for it.

6. Get ready to start working

When you go to the office, there's a transition: a time and a place that separates your work and home life. On your way there, your brain goes into work mode, you forget about home matters and you start thinking about work.

That time and change of location disappear when you work from home. Saving the time you used to spend traveling to work, stuck in traffic or wedged in like a sardine on public transport, is hugely beneficial – but you do lose that natural transition.

When you work from home, you can stumble straight to your desk still bleary-eyed. But if even your face isn't ready to start work, how can your mind be? Being physically sat in front of your computer doesn't mean you're truly there.

Remote working doesn't normally give you that natural transition that allows your mind to reframe itself, but you can create one. That transition will tell your brain it needs to get into work mode.

One of the most popular tips on remote working, which you'll see in lots of articles on the subject, is: "Get out of your pajamas and get dressed for work." Well, I'm not going to tell you to get out of your pajamas if you like working in them. Why should you? No one is going to judge you. There's no dress code when you work from home. But if you have a videocall, you should probably change at least the top half of your teddy bear PJs.

This widely-circulated piece of advice is easily explained. Taking off your pajamas, taking a shower and putting on regular clothes serves as a transition that prepares us to start working. When you take off those cute, comfy teddy bears (or stripes, if you're old-school), you're telling your brain it's time to switch from "home mode" to "work mode", even though you're still at home.

What other ways can you make that transition?

Any small detail can work to send the signal to your brain that it's time to start working. You should do it several times in a row so that your mind associates that action with getting to work. Create your own rituals.

Here are a few ideas:

- Take a shower and get dressed in regular clothes (I know someone who puts their tie on over their pajamas).
- Have your morning coffee in that motivational mug you got for your

birthday. Only use it when you're working, to make the association clearer.

- Go into a different room.
- Listen to different music especially for working.
- Mark out an area for you to work in. It could be a simple line on the floor that you consciously cross in order to begin working.

You can do one or more things to let your brain know it's time for work.

What rituals or transitions will you use to get yourself ready to work?

7. Take control of your schedule

When you're working remotely, you realize you've never been so in charge of your schedule. In the office, lots of people spend their days going from meeting to meeting (and so on and so forth). And between meetings, maybe your colleague catches you in the hallway and decides to take the opportunity to ask you about something that clearly wasn't important enough to email you about – and, of course, you have to stand there for a few minutes listening. When you finally sit down, your boss says: "Hey, this report…" and proceeds to talk about something that only just occurred to him, and if you hadn't been there at that precise moment, he never would've mentioned it to you.

With remote working, these kinds of interruptions disappear – at least, for the most part. Of course, you'll have some meetings, but you'll see they are much less frequent than when you were at the office. With some luck, you'll only have the ones that are necessary and indispensable. Most of them will also get straight to the point and be more productive. There will always be exceptions, of course, and I can't promise you that all your remote work meetings will be a success – but they will be less frequent, and better.

As for your colleague from the hallway, you

won't be bumping into him in your hallway at home (I hope not, anyway – horror movie vibes). And your boss won't bother calling you every single time he has a great idea (we hope).

At the office, your schedule simply fills up – sometimes without your input. You lose control. But when you start working remotely, you have to take control of it yourself. More than ever before, you'll be the person responsible for filling in the blank pages of every day, week and month. You'll have to take responsibility for your planning.

Sounds good, right? At last: control over what you do and when you do it.

However, taking on that responsibility can be overwhelming. Why? Because you aren't used to managing your own schedule; even if you thought you were doing it, others were doing it for you.

If you don't know where to start, either because you have so much to do, you think you don't have enough, or simply because that blank planner sheet is scaring you…now is the time to take control of your time: your day, your week, your month.

If you've never done it before, it's an exercise that requires some practice and a little trial and error to adapt to what works best for you, but you'll soon pick it up.

The following tips will help you with planning. Remember that now, more than ever, you are the master of your own schedule. Be aware of that and accept that responsibility.

8. Find out when you're most productive

We're not equally productive over the eight hours that a working day normally lasts, nor is everyone equally productive at the same times. Books and productivity gurus can tell us till they're blue in the face that great leaders and CEOs get up at 5am and take on the day – take that with a grain of salt. That does not work for everyone. We're all different, and some people – like me – find themselves sleepy and irritable if they get up at 5am, or even 6, and the feeling lasts all day. Some of us are more productive, creative and efficient and other times of day.

You'll have to work out your best time for working.

To help you do this, I recommend that for at least a week, you keep a productivity journal where you note down what you're doing at what time, how long it takes you, your level of productivity, the type of task it is, and notes on things like distractions and so on.

Doing this for five days will give you a better idea of your biological work rhythm, and the external factors that affect your performance.

You might be wondering – why work when I'm most productive when I get paid the same either way? Well – for exactly that reason. For the majority of jobs, what matters is that you fulfil your roles and tasks. The amount of time you spend sitting at your computer is irrelevant. Now that you're working remotely and your boss can't see you, anyway. If you can fulfil your duties in six hours instead of eight, why not do so and spend the other two hours taking a walk, having a coffee with a friend, watching YouTube or getting other jobs done? And your boss won't mind, because you did your work.

If your work days tend to stretch beyond the usual eight hours, you need this tool to help you optimize your schedule and find that work-life balance.

Once you have worked out when you do each task and how you feel at each moment, you'll have some info for creating a schedule that suits your needs. Get to know yourself to find out what the best times are to undertake each type of task. Various external factors will have an impact on this, too, such as your surroundings, coordinating with other people, and so on.

The following is an example of how my day usually works to optimize my productivity to the full:

- I start the morning by undertaking a task that doesn't require too much mental effort or creativity (like I said, I get up still half-asleep).

- Then, I plan out the most demanding tasks: the ones I really have to think about, be creative, or talk to people.

- After I eat, my energy dips again, so I do another straightforward task.

- I end the day on the jobs I like most and find most entertaining. Even when I'm tired, it's not hard to do something I enjoy.

This is just an example: your pace might be very different from mine, and a different plan may be better for you. To find out, fill in the Productivity Journal, which you can [download here](http://carmencorral.com/productivity-journal). This will help tell you not just when to plan different tasks, but what times to start and finish work.

Bear your environment in mind while doing this, as well as the requirements of the company you work for (they may need you to be available from nine to five) and other family or personal commitments and obligations (such as picking the kids up from school).

Don't let anyone tell you you have to get up at 5am to be productive. Try it for yourself and decide if it works for you. Don't let anyone tell you you have to finish work at 5pm, either, or once the kids get back from school. I don't doubt that working with children in the house presents challenges, but that doesn't mean it's impossible – and if it suits your needs, then why not? Make the most of the flexible hours of remote working that your personal situation allows you to plan out.

I recommend that you keep the productivity journal for more than a week, to give you more information to help you get to know and value yourself better. And you don't have to stop doing it at any particular point – if you want, you can keep filling it in every day for weeks and months. It will help you get organized and improve your productivity.

9. Create a routine

We are creatures of habit and routine. And you can take that from me, someone who hates routine.

If, on the other hand, you are someone who likes to have a daily routine and stick to it, you'll be in your element once you find it. Now that you're working remotely and are in charge of your schedule, it will be easier to adjust your routine to how you want it. It will be somewhat difficult at first to get used to new habits, and I challenge you to be a little adventurous and try different options before establishing a definitive routine.

If, like me, you break out in hives when you hear the word "routine", let me explain to you why it's important to have one. If you prefer, and it makes you feel better, then call it something else: habits, system, structure.

Establishing a routine means you don't have to make constant decisions about what to do and when. Every day, I get up, have breakfast in the kitchen, take a shower, then start work. I start by catching up and answering emails, and at around eleven, I have a coffee and carry on. I don't have to wake up and make a decision about what to do today: shower first, or breakfast? I just start the day on autopilot, with no effort or energy required for those little decisions that sometimes just lead me to procrastinate: "I'd better stay in bed a few more minutes while I decide whether to have breakfast or shower first."

If you're a lover of flexibility and improvising in your day-to-day life, you need a routine more than anyone. The most creative and innovative painters say it's necessary to know the rules in order to break them. You need a routine (or a system), in order to ignore it. You don't have to follow it strictly, just have it as a reference, a structure.

Whereas I tell people who like routine to try different options, I tell you that rather than trying one after the other, you should give each one a little time to be able to assess them properly.

To create a routine, use the productivity journal (http://carmencorral.com/productivity-journal). Basing yourself off it, see how you feel about the different combinations of places, times and tasks.

For example, start the day by going over today's schedule at the kitchen table with a coffee. Mid-morning, go to that local coffee place you like so much and that inspire you to get creative in your work – plus, the coffee is delicious (watch the caffeine! ;))

The good thing about routines is that we settle

into them almost without realizing. The bad thing about them is that we settle into them almost without realizing. That's right – it's both bad and good. It's easy to get used to doing certain things at the same time of day, in the same place, but is that really what's best for us?

That's why filling out the [Productivity Journal](http://carmencorral.com/productivity-journal) will help you work out which routines you're not interested in sticking to, and help you get into a routine that fits your needs best.

10. Escape your routine

If you feel tied down by so much routine, like I do, then get out of it – but only once you've created it. If you love routine, escape it from time to time, too. It may seem contradictory for me to first tell you to make one and then to get out of it. Let me explain.

As we've seen, creating your routine helps you to focus and gives you a structure to base your days around. Now, you need a little spontaneity. Some people need it more than others, and to a lesser or greater extent.

Escaping your routine will help to keep you awake, creative, and recharged with energy. It will enable you to see things from a different perspective. It's ideal when you feel stuck in a rut, down a one-way street on some task you're doing. If you need inspiration, give yourself a break or work from somewhere different.

Now that you're remote working, it's much easier to escape your daily routine than when you were spending 8 hours in the office, day after day, sitting in the same chair.

Give yourself a change of scenery and spend a few hours a week working from a café, a coworking space, or simply your lounge at home. Or take a few hours off in the middle of the week to walk through the park, have coffee with a friend, or read a book. Getting out of routine doesn't just mean working somewhere else; it could also be working on a different task, or taking a break. It means doing something different from what you do every other day.

So, if you're a lover of routine and you like always knowing what you're going to do next, you can plan to escape your routine on a specific day, and write down in your weekly schedule "get out of routine". Seem paradoxical? Maybe – if you prefer, call it "change of scenery". Do something different from every other day. And preferably, make this something different each week. For example, if you plan to get out of your routine every Wednesday from 12pm to 2pm by going to a café, that's great – you can do the same thing the following week, and the one after that, but try to swap it for something new and different before it simply becomes another routine. This will help keep that "out of a rut" freshness going.

This is a good chance to try new options, places and habits for working that you can then incorporate into your daily or weekly routine. Check to see if anything new is working well for you.

Incorporate an escape from your routine into your weekly routine.

11. Change positions

At the office, you probably have a good chair to spend the eight hours of your working day sitting in. Maybe it wasn't an ergonomic chair, but at least it was an office chair.

Now that you're working from home, you may not have an office with your own desk and chair. That doesn't mean that your health needs to suffer; you don't want to end up with back pain.

Out of the office, you have a big advantage. You have more options than just one desk and chair. You can work from anywhere in your home. That means you don't have to spend eight hours sitting in the same seat. Change places, chairs and positions.

Changing position during your working day is more beneficial than sitting in a good chair for eight hours straight every day.

Use the breakfast bar to work standing up for a while. Move from your office chair to a kitchen one for an hour. Check your emails on the couch. Your body will thank you for the change in posture.

Do you think you can only work from one place in the house? That you won't be able to concentrate anywhere else? Don't knock it before you try it. You don't need to spend hours in that place – but try it for a while for a few days in a row.

The following is my own routine for changing places and positions. I normally start working in bed, while drinking tea. I know this isn't for everyone (working while in bed, that is – not the tea). I usually do it when the tasks I need to do involve more clicking than typing (which isn't so comfortable from that position). Then, I sit in a chair at the table, which can be one in a café or a kitchen or dining chair. In some places around the world, I've even worked while sitting on the floor. I have my preferences depending on time of day, but above all, depending on the type of task I need to undertake. When I'm going to be writing text, I need a chair with a backrest and a table I can put my laptop on.

I can tell you that since I've been working remotely, I have had no more back pain. Well – only on the occasion that I've not followed my own advice, and spent all day sitting in the same position.

Now, it's up to you to find what works for you. Perhaps working in the kitchen in the morning when there's no one else home, and then in your home office when everyone gets in?

Wherever you do it, remember: don't spend the whole day sitting in one chair. Move around, and your back will thank you for it.

12. Rest

Take breaks. Just because you're working remotely, doesn't mean you can't have your mid-morning coffee break or take a half-hour for lunch.

Stopping for a coffee is easy, but what about food? Eating in front of the computer and pretending you're working isn't the most productive thing to do. You might think you're saving a lot of time by eating and working at the same time, but you're really not. It's hard to get much done while you're eating. It's impossible to type. You might be able to read, but how long is it taking you? Longer than if you were just reading and not eating.

Take your lunch break to eat, relax, and enjoy the taste of your food. After all, how long does that take you: fifteen, twenty minutes? Sometimes, probably even less.

During your breaks, get up, walk around the kitchen, go to the bathroom, around all the rooms in the house, take a walk around the block or take the chance to go buy some fresh bread.

Getting out of your chair will help you relax and recharge. If you're doing a job that requires creativity, a rest can help you come back not only stronger, but with a new idea or two, too.

Take breaks and be aware that you're doing so. Working from home can give you the feeling that you've worked non-stop all day. This particularly happens when you make your working day so flexible that work gets interwoven with personal errands, more work, personal life and family commitments, a little more work, and a few hours of you-time to round off the day. You may feel as if you worked all day even when you didn't, because you took little time to do other things.

When you take breaks from work, whether it's five minutes for a coffee or a whole hour to go grocery shopping, make sure your mind registers it as a break from work. If you find that hard to do mentally, help your brain out by marking those hours on your calendar with the word "break" or the activity. Highlight them in a different color, so that you can see at a glance that you didn't spend the whole day working.

Running errands and doing chores aren't exactly a "break", but they are a break from work. It's a change in activity, which means you stop for a while, and your brain registers it as a break from what you were doing.

Even though you come back from the gym physically tired, that hour you took to work out was a break for your mind. What you have to decide is whether the activities you do during your breaks help you recharge you to keep on working or not. For example, working right after getting back from the gym is hard for some people, while others feel energized and ready to take on the rest of their working day.

13. Set boundaries for bosses and clients

Just because you're working remotely doesn't mean you're working 24/7, nor that you always have to be available. Your flexibility is decided by you, and you may sometimes decide to work the weekend or into the early hours of the morning – but don't let your bosses, colleagues or clients get used to it. Keep that flexibility for yourself.

I'm going to let you in on a secret. I hope none of my clients are reading this. Every now and again, a client will email me on a Saturday. And that's fine: they decided to work over the weekend. I usually read my emails the same day, even on Saturdays and Sundays (I can't help myself), but I don't have to do that. Even if I read it, I don't answer till Monday – especially if it's a new client. Why? Because it's a way to let them know off the bat that I won't be available weekends, and that they will have to wait until Monday.

At first, I would reply the same day, even on Saturdays, Sundays and holidays. Until one day, when a client sent me a message late on a Friday. He was so used to me responding the same or next day, that on Sunday night he followed up with another message to check that I had gotten the first one. He was simply surprised not to have received a response. Fortunately, in this case, it didn't damage our relationship (though it could have done) and I still work with that client today.

Some people don't recognize weekends, holidays and working days – they just keep working. And that's up to them. You can work every day at all hours, too, if you want. But I advise you not to bite off more than you can chew and end up getting your boss, clients or colleagues used to you being available round the clock. Because today, you may be willing to reply to an email at 11pm, but tomorrow you might not want to do so simply because you set a precedent.

If you have to, set days and times when you will and won't be available. Communication is very important in remote working, and agreements can be necessary to narrow down that flexibility.

If you pick up the kids every day at 4pm, you have no reason to keep that a secret from your boss. But if he always calls at that time, you'll pick up the phone annoyed every time: "he always, *always,* calls right then". He probably wouldn't mind calling you at 4:30, instead, but if he doesn't know then he doesn't know.

Set your working hours and, if you need to, tell people.

33 consejos para el TELETRAJO

14. Adapt productivity techniques to your needs

If you're reading this book, you may have read books on productivity before. If you devour this kind of literature, searching for the master key to getting more done and being better organized, then breathe. You won't find the whole answer written in books. But before you stop reading around the subject, read carefully what I am about to tell you.

There are many techniques, tools and secrets to productivity: getting up at 5am, the Pomodoro Technique, Priority Matrix, GTD (Getting Things Done) ...

How can you follow them all? It's not advisable to – or even possible. Some actually contradict each other.

Everyone is different, so how could it work the same for everyone? Different things work for different people. That's why, while it's good to read up around productivity, tools and technique, you have to adapt them to you and your needs.

When we adopt other people's productivity techniques, we think they'll definitely work for us. Why? Because it's in the books, because other people say it's worked, because we think it's a silver bullet: a secret recipe for making everything we have to do totally effortless.

But what really happens? Well, many of those tools don't work, because everyone is different. We try something, we don't stick to it, and we despair. "Why isn't it working for me? I'll never be productive, I'm a disaster."

Some techniques are simply very hard – they require so much effort to implement in our lives that we end up failing and feeling frustrated. If something is really that difficult for you, it's probably not right for you right now.

If you think something might suit you, try it. Give it a chance, and if it doesn't work for you, then don't feel bad for not being able to stick to that productivity technique that "all the big CEOs are using".

You don't have to follow these techniques to a T – adapt them to you and to what works best for you.

But don't kid yourself, either. Don't tell yourself that a tip isn't working well for you when really, you just don't want to do it. Try things more than once before discarding them. You need to adapt to some techniques before they start showing results.

15. Schedule your tasks

It's very useful to make a list of your pending tasks. First of all, this will help you to remember what you have to do, and free your mind from thoughts such as "I must remember to do that job", which can keep bugging you until you either complete the task or note it down.

A to-do list where you check off tasks as you complete them is a basic productivity tool. But let's go a step further, because the usefulness of such a list is limited.

Instead of writing a task down on a simple list, you note, write it in your schedule along with the day you're going to do it and the time it will take you to complete it, not only will you not forget to do it but you'll also have a commitment to do so. You're closer to completing tasks that have a date and time assigned to them on your calendar.

This will give you a more "3D" view of your task. Not only do you know what you need to do, but you can also estimate how long it will take you. Not all tasks are equal in duration and complexity, and a simple list can make it look as though they are.

If you've completed the Productivity Journal

(www.carmencorral.com/productivity-journal), you'll know your best time for doing each type of task and you can add them to your schedule accordingly.

Putting them into your schedule doesn't mean they're an inescapable commitment. Be flexible if you need to be. If you sit down to work and feel that it's not the best time to do the job you'd noted down on your calendar, do a different one. Move that task to another space on your calendar. This way it won't stay outstanding, but you push it back to do later at a specific time.

Here are the advantages of using this method:

- You're more committed to completing the task as it's noted in your schedule for a certain date and time

- Better planning

- It enables you to see how long each task takes you

- A clearer vision of your daily, weekly and monthly organization

I also like to note down in the same agenda (I use Google calendar) the things I do outside of work. I do this in a different color: blue for the spaces I fill in with work tasks, orange for personal and leisure.

I also have a list of outstanding tasks. I create this first, when I do my weekly meeting, and then I add the tasks on the list to my weekly schedule. Some remain on the list as outstanding; these are the ones that don't fit into my weekly schedule.

I note down directly into my schedule, without going through the list first, any appointments, meetings and commitments that already have a fixed date, even if it's in a month's time.

Personally, I'm extremely flexible when it comes to moving and relocating tasks within my schedule. Almost every day, I change their order. You might wonder if it makes sense to do it this way if there is so much flexibility – why bother to give them a date and time if I end up moving them around? Yes, it does make sense and is logical. It's easier to be flexible this way, because I can clearly see how long it takes me to do each task, and how they fit into the hours I have for working.

.

16. Focus on what's essential

There's something that most authors who write about productivity agree on, although they call it different things: doing what's important, establishing priorities, focusing on what's essential. With a few variations, nuances and techniques, what they all tell us is that we should identify what's most important in our work (applying this to our lives, too) and then do it.

Identify what you need to do to achieve your goals. These can be numeric goals, with a concrete result that must be attained, but they can also be qualitative – such as, for example, providing better customer service. Not everything you do every day is important – at least, not equally important. Work out what's essential in order to achieve your objectives.

Those important, essential tasks are the nerve center of your job.

Every day, do one of those essential tasks: put them into your schedule ahead of anything else. Other tasks can be slotted around them like accessories.

Focusing on what's important and essential will not only enable you to work more efficiently, but you'll also feel that you are more efficient.

Dedicating a few hours each day to what's really significant in your work, to the nerve center of your job, will make you feel better than if you only spend time on side quests that aren't as important and don't bring much to your work's purpose.

When you identify what your essential tasks are, you'll realize that some of the things you usually "just do" are actually useless. Eliminate them from your schedule. If it's a task you share with other people on your team, whether that's doing them or just giving them the results, tell them. Let them know what your opinion is, and why you think the task is dispensable. They probably actually agree with you that it can go.

17. Work in blocks

Working in blocks means gathering together a certain type of task and doing them all together. For example, giving yourself one hour to answer the emails in your inbox or to make phone calls. It's more efficient to answer all your emails together than to reply to one, and then another five minutes later, and then another an hour after that.

Think about those seconds it takes you to find the files you need to start a new task. Or about opening and logging into a new app on your computer. They may only be seconds, but if you're constantly changing tasks, they add up over the course of the day and become minutes. Maybe you're thinking about keeping all the programs and documents you'll need over the course of the day open at once on your computer, but I don't recommend it, because it'll be distracting and take you longer to find the tab you need.

Just like your computer's operating system, your brain needs some time to respond to new commands. It normally takes quite a few moments, or even minutes, to get focused on a new task. Working in blocks is more efficient, because you save the time and effort your brain needs to concentrate every time you change from one task to another.

It will also be easier to organize yourself if you work in different places. For example, you can take all the phone calls you need to make, and make them between twelve and one, which is the quietest time in your house, and because the coffee shop you like to work from in the mornings isn't quiet enough to make phone calls to clients. That would be a better place to reply to any unanswered emails.

In many cases, it makes sense to group by thematic block rather than type of task. So instead of making blocks according to whether it's email, phone calls, and so on, you make them based around a single project.

18. Take things little by little

Have you heard of the Pomodoro productivity technique? It's very simple; it consists of working for twenty-five minutes, taking a five-minute break, and so on and so forth. This technique marks out short periods of time, which enables us to concentrate better and avoid distractions. Who isn't capable of working for twenty-five minutes in a row without checking their Facebook or even their email? If you know that in twenty-five minutes' time, you'll get a five-minute break, it's easier to focus on what you have to.

However, this technique does have some drawbacks. There are tasks that require more than twenty-five minutes of concentration, and taking a break right when you've hit your stride isn't the best idea.

The best thing is to adapt this technique to your needs. For me, for example, when I have to write, twenty-five minutes aren't enough. Just when I've settled into writing, the break timer goes off what seems like a few minutes later, and all my inspiration evaporates.

Adapt the length of time to each task. When you fill out your productivity journal, you'll see how much time you really spend on each job. Set your break timer for that long.

If you have a very large project, divide it into mini-projects to make it more approachable. If a task is very long, divide it into parts and decide where you'll go up to and how long you'll spend on that.

It's typically hard to concentrate for more than one hour at a time, but sometimes we get into a "flow" and we can go on for hours. If that happens, don't stop if you don't want to. Keep working as long as it's flowing. Be flexible with your timings. Then, take a longer break: ten minutes per hour of work is a good rule of thumb.

Take things little by little. Sitting down in front of a huge task can be overwhelming. *Where do I start?* That simple question can paralyze you. Instead of starting that big task or project at random, in any place, take the time to break it down into smaller tasks.

19. Don't obsess over productivity

Exactly that: don't get obsessed with being the most productive person ever. I don't mean don't work to improve and make every day shorter as well as better – what I mean is, don't blame yourself if you're not using your time to the full.

Just think: when you were in the office, your performance was basically measured by the eight hours you spent sitting at your desk. Sure, there were goals and results to think about, but when you were in the office from nine to five, nobody doubted that you were working. Now that you're not there, you're the first one to start doubting that you're really giving it your all and doing what's expected of you.

Now that you're working remotely, measuring your performance is different. No one knows if you're sitting at a desk for eight hours, and for the first time, your performance is being measure by the work that gets done. It's your responsibility to do it. It (finally) no longer matters how long you sit at your desk for. Now, you have to show you're getting results and fulfilling your role.

Many people, when they start out remote working, put so much pressure on their own shoulders about how long they should be working for (sitting at their desk) and/or the amount of work they should be producing. This is a kind of overcompensation: "Now that the boss can't see me, I'm going to do more than I was doing before, so he doesn't start doubting my performance."

Dear bosses, if you're reading this, you should know that this happens a lot more often than the opposite ("Now that the boss can't see me, I don't have to work so much").

Thinking that your superior – or even your colleagues – are questioning whether or not you're working is all in your head. You have no reason to think they're doubting you. Are you doubting them?

Be responsible about what you do, when you do it, and how you do it, and you'll have nothing to worry about or any reason to obsess over what others think about your performance.

20. Distract the distractions and interrupt the interruptions

- Facebook

- "I haven't read the news today, what's happening in the world?"

- "I haven't heard from Anna in a while, I'll WhatsApp her."

- "I feel like another coffee; I'm getting up to make one."

- Instagram

- *Beep, beep!* "Who's messaging me?"

- "Surely it's time for a cookie."

We are surrounded by distractions. Some are a few feet away, others are right in our faces, muscling in on our workspace.

All these distractions have something in common: they give us immediate gratification with minimal effort. That's why they are so powerful, and so hard to resist. On a biological level, when we give in to these activities, our brains release dopamine, which gives us a pleasant sensation. This is the same substance and process involved in addiction.

Social media is today's number one distraction. It may be a tool for work, but it's even harder to know when it's actually useful and when it's just another distraction. But it's far from the only distraction lurking around us.

That succulent piece of chocolate cake left over from yesterday is calling to you from the kitchen. You can't stop thinking about it and your stomach is growling. *So hungry*, you think. *Can't work like this.* In reality, you only ate a couple of hours ago. And even if you hadn't, you can still work while you're hungry if you just don't think about it. Focus on what you have to do, and hunger will leave you alone; focus on hunger, and you'll forget what it is you have to do. Stick the cake, cookies or apples on a waiting list – they'll still be in the kitchen when you finish work. And they'll be the perfect reward for having completed what you were doing, or simply for having dodged the distraction.

Distract your distractions, and set yourself a time when you'll pay them attention. Meanwhile, focus on work. It'll be easier to do, knowing that in an hour, you'll have five minutes to check your Facebook. If, while you're working, you start thinking about things you want to look up online or a friend you want to catch up with, just note it down on a piece of paper (or on your computer) to do when you've finished your task and it's time to give your "distractions" a little airtime. You might think that it'll take you the same amount of time to type out a simple message to your friend as it will to write down a note to do it later. That may be true, but once you give in to that distraction, it takes over your time. You open WhatsApp, and now that you have your phone in your hand, you start checking out the latest on Instagram, too.

Mute your notifications on your phone so they don't distract you. Or, if you don't need your phone for work, go one better and leave it in another room so it doesn't keep tempting you to pick it up. Set yourself a length of time you'll be working for, concentrate properly for half an hour, or an hour, it's up to you. What could be so urgent that it can't wait an hour? If you're waiting on an important call, mute everything except calls.

Schedule yourself some time to dedicate to those distractions. This could be five or ten minutes every hour.

If you get interrupted at work, whether by a person or by one of those distractions: interrupt it. Say: "I'm sorry, I can't deal with you right now, in X minutes I'll be finished and I'll be all yours." Say it to your kids when they get home, to Facebook when you're tempted to open it, to the cookies waiting for you in the kitchen.

21. Make tools your biggest ally

IT tools are your best friend; don't turn them into your worst enemy. And I say this in particular to the technophobes among you.

Think of each new tool you use as a person you just met and are getting to know. Don't expect too much, don't make assumptions, don't judge too quickly. Just like a new friend, simply spend some time getting to know it.

Only once you do that with a tool will you be able to know what you can expect from it and get out of it. Again, like with a friend; because we count on different friends for different things, right? We go to certain friends for their insight on a potential new job, and to others when we want advice on a family matter. We might go for coffee with some, and for a weekend dinner with others. But first, we need some time to get to know each other to find out what it is we can expect from each friend.

That's what you should do with work tools. There is no one perfect tool for everything. You'll need several different ones, and even then you may find some gap that no tool can quite fill. Don't seek perfection in a tool, just accept it and use it if it's helpful to you. And if it's not, don't. It doesn't have to form part of your work arsenal if it's not useful to you.

What happens when you expect too much of a tool? Well, the same thing that happens when you expect too much of a friend and that friend doesn't meet your expectations: they end up disappointing you. Sometimes, they can even end up becoming your worst enemy.

If you're a little reticent when it comes to technology, don't let it become your enemy; technology is here to help and make things easier, but you have to be patient and spend a little time getting to grips with it.

Be patient with yourself when learning to use a new tool; don't discard it straight away because you're "not getting on with it". Don't make them your enemy without giving them the chance to become your best friend.

Learning to use a new tool takes some time, and makes work slower at first. But only at first — then, it should make things quicker and more efficient. That's the aim when using a tool. It's necessary, and you can't avoid that initial stage.

Imagine an intern joined your work team and you were the person charged with showing them the ropes. At first, you have to invest a little time in explaining things, and your own work may take a hit, but once they've learned, they can help you and together you'll work faster and better. The same thing applies to a new tool: except you're the one learning. Take it slowly.

22. Don't lose yourself in tools

Now that you know that tools are your friends and great work colleagues, it's time to choose your staff – sorry, I mean, choose your tools.

One of the first questions people tend to ask me about remote working is: "what tools do you use?". And by that, people mean IT tools and apps. There tends to be more interest in them than in the methods, techniques, tactics, or whatever you want to call it, of getting organized and general work processes. Maybe it's because we all have the naïve hope that some IT tool will be the magic key to resolving everything.

But tools are just that: tools. A carpenter has a hammer to help him put nails in. But if he doesn't know how to hold the nail or hit with the hammer, it's useless to him. However, if he knows how to hammer in a nail, then even without the hammer he could do it with a different tool – like a stone, for example. Of course, the hammer is much more useful and efficient, but it's possible to get the job done without it.

The same applies to IT tools. A powerful messaging app for remote teams isn't much use if the people using it don't know how to communicate effectively.

Don't lose yourself in tools and apps; there are so many out there, and many of them promise to work wonders. Explore some of them – not all – and stick with just those that are indispensable to helping you do your job. Working with multiple tools at once requires extra effort, which could end up defeating the object of using them.

It may be that your company or clients require you to use certain tools – in that case, you'll simply have to adapt. Avoid making your life complicated by using other tools for your personal and professional organization unless you really need them.

So, how do you choose a tool? Before picking one, ask yourself:

- What do I need? What do I want to achieve?

- How do I want this tool to help me? Specify what functions it should have.

Once you've tried the new tool, ask yourself:

- Does it do what I need it to (does it have the functions mentioned above)? Analyze which requirements it fulfils and which it doesn't, and order these by importance. It may not do something in exactly the way you hoped it would, but it might do it in a way that helps you work with the tool.

- Does using this tool help me do X thing (insert your answer to the first question of "what do I need?")? This could be about getting better results, saving time being better organized, and so on.

If it doesn't fulfil your basic requirements and do what you need it to, discard it straight away. If it does what you need it to and fulfils most of your requirements, but not all, assess whether it's worth continuing your search for an app that's more closely suited to your needs, or if it's worth sticking with this one. Remember: the perfect tool doesn't exist.

And since I know you'll still be wondering which tools you should use, here are some useful ones. Remember – you have to decide for yourself if any one tool is right for you.

Videocalling:

- Zoom
- Google Meet
- Skype

Document sharing and online working:

- Google Drive
- Dropbox
- Office 365

Project management:

- Trello
- Asana

Time management:

- Rescue Time
- Toggl

Messages:

- Slack

I would like to include a special mention for WhatsApp. It's a terrible tool to use for work. Messages are totally unstructured and information is hard to retrieve later. I advise against using WhatsApp for work. It should only be used for what it is: instant messaging, for example, to let someone know you've sent them an email they need to read.

23. Communicate more clearly

With remote work, the way you communicate changes. Many people make excuses not to work remotely because communication won't be the same. And it's true that it will be different; but that's all. Just different – not necessarily worse. I promise you that sometimes, it'll be even better.

These are the most noteworthy changes:

- There will be more written and less verbal communication.

- Some body language is lost.

- There will be less connection with and proximity to people you work with – but that's not necessarily a bad thing. You probably won't become best friends with your colleagues this way, but you won't get any of that typical office drama that comes from being in each other's pockets, either.

To communicate, you'll need various tools: phone, email, and other apps and software provided by your company or clients or that you agree on with your colleagues. Don't go crazy with the number of communication tools you use; using a lot at once can often cause more communication problems than it solves.

— *I didn't get your email.*
— *That's because I didn't send it to your email, I sent it via Skype.*
— *Oh, I don't check my Skype every day.*

Agree on what you'll use to communicate. For example, always use the same videocalling tool to avoid confusion whereby some people are waiting for a meeting to start on Zoom while others are waiting on Skype. It's also easier for everyone to get to grips with just one app. If you want to have a backup in case your usual one goes down, keep it as just that: a backup. Clearly specify that it's a spare tire that you'll only use if your regular one isn't working, and with prior notice.

Communication needs to be clearer. However, this doesn't mean more extensive. You have to strike a balance between providing all of the necessary information and providing it in a way that's concise.

Avoid excess information – it's counterproductive. If you want someone to read the instructions on a job, then get straight to the point and say what's essential. If you go overboard with your information, writing emails that look like essays, your recipient will get bored and end up skim-reading it.

There will be more written communication. This has some upsides – for example, you'll be able to go back to it and reread it later. Once you get used to this, to having nearly all your information in writing, you can end up skipping taking notes in meetings or during phone calls. But even if someone tells you they'll send something to you in writing afterward, you should still make note of what is said, because sometimes that email never comes, or the content of it isn't quite accurate.

Always check messages before sending them, to make sure you're providing the necessary information in the proper way. Spelling or grammatical mistakes can totally change the meaning of a message.

24. Limit your number of meetings

With remote working, you'll notice that meetings are less frequent and shorter – at least, they should be. Many companies suffer from meetingitis. Sometimes they even know it but do nothing to remedy it.

Meetings can limit that time flexibility you're finally enjoying. If your whole team is remote working, the others will feel the same way. So, to avoid that limitation on your newly-acquired flexibility, do everything in your power to reduce the number of meetings you have.

Meetings should also be shorter, as they're a little more difficult via a screen than in person.

Now is the perfect time to limit meetings. If a company starting remote work doesn't realize that, they may fall into the temptation of continuing the same dynamic of calling endless, interminable meetings that don't benefit anyone or make work any easier.

If you're not absolutely essential at a meeting, and you can say no, do so. You probably won't miss anything, and no one will miss you either. If you're the one calling the meeting, ask yourself twice: does this need a meeting, or could you coordinate this with the other person/people involved in another way? Who is really needed at this meeting? Could you leave out any of the people you were planning to call in?

An online meeting that lasts more than an hour is very long, and very often could probably be shortened.

25. Make the most out of videocalling

Videocalling still does not come naturally to most of us. Sitting in a conference room surrounded by your colleagues is something you know well, because you've done it countless times before. And not just for your company; you've sat in family gatherings (probably around a table piled high with food) and talked. But we're not so used to video. We have less experience communication through this new, screen-based medium – at least, for now.

With practice, we'll learn to manage videocalling as well as we manage in person. Remember to take it as training, and learn from your mistakes so you can get better.

When I talk about making the most out of videocalling, I'm not talking about multitasking while others are talking (quite the contrary). I'm talking about learning to get along with this new tool that's here to stay. Today it could be a semi-informal chat with your colleagues, but tomorrow it could be a videocall with an important client to close a big deal, or a job interview to get that promotion you so badly want and deserve.

These are some things to bear in mind; you'll come across others for yourself. Make note of them to help you improve:

The pace of videocalling is different. If it's hard to pay attention in a face-to-face meeting, it's even harder on a videocall. This is one of the reasons why it's more important than ever to organize meetings with an agenda and with speaking time for everyone. It's best for one person to head up the meeting, so they can ensure everything goes smoothly. It may seem inevitable that everyone will speak at once, but it should be avoided at all costs during videocalls. It's inefficient in person, but you'll see that in videocalls, it's unbearable.

When you're speaking, rather than looking at the screen, look up at the camera. That might sound like the same thing, but it's not; the effect is totally different. If you're not looking at the camera, you're not establishing eye contact with other speakers. It will look as if you're not looking at the people you're talking to, even though you are. Locate the camera on your computer and look at it when it's your turn to speak. This will give you eye contact with all participants. It's pretty unavoidable for your eyes to drift down to the screen where you are your colleagues are. A good trick is to make the videocalling window smaller and move it up near your webcam, so that even if your gaze drifts, it's still close to the camera.

Get to know the tool you'll be using before the call. Ideally, always (or nearly always) use the same tool, so that everyone at the meeting can be familiar with it. In particular, if it's a meeting with several people, it's important that they all take the necessary time to get to grips with the tool before the meeting starts. If it's the first time you've used that tool as a group, you can do a test call before the meeting to try it out. This will help show you how the platform works without interrupting the meeting itself.

If you're calling a meeting and some people can attend in person while others can only do video, move it online for everyone. Managing a meeting with some of the attendees in the room and some online is difficult as well as possibly unsatisfactory for all attendees (especially those online). If you've ever been at one of these mixed meetings, you will have noticed that technical problems often arise: someone online can't hear the people in the room, or vice versa. Internet connection can cause a delay. The person or people online tend to participate much less – even if they power through technical difficulties, it's harder for them to get a word in edgeways. Ultimately, they are not there in the room with you. Even if most of the attendees are present and only one person can't be there, try to have the meeting completely online. You'll see that things flow much better this way.

26. Relate to others

We have already talked about how communication is different now: not necessarily better or worse, but different. Something most teams who start remote working notice is that their relationships are much less close. This can be an advantage, because it prevents conflicts that can arise in the close quarters of a workplace. However, a cohesive work team needs more than purely work-related communication.

In the office, when you get in on Monday morning and are taking off your coat, you chat to your colleagues about what you did over the weekend. They tell you what they made for dinner with friends or what movie they went to see yesterday, and you make a mental note to go see it yourself. And during the week, you chat about your everyday lives. You know how many kids your department workmates have, and even some of their names and ages.

It's harder to have these interactions in a remote working environment. It won't happen in the same spontaneous way that it does every day in an office. You have to engineer this kind of communication, and use mechanisms to get to know the people you're working with to foster a closer relationship.

It's not about knowing your colleagues' private lives for the sake of it. The aim is to establish a connection with them and cultivate trust and camaraderie between you.

Here are some simple tricks for encouraging closer communication:

- Use emojis in messages with your team, between colleagues. They lend a touch of closeness to the dialog.

- Ask them how they are, and other, more specific questions about what you know about that person.

- Talk about yourself a little.

- A simple comment about how sunny it was over the weekend should be enough to establish a connection. Avoid complaining, though – nobody likes a whiner.

- Organize videocalls so you can see each other's faces.

- Take a few minutes in meetings to talk

about yourself and your lives outside work. But avoid letting the meeting run over the scheduled time unnecessarily, or the attendees could blame it on those few minutes you spent talking about things other than work. If you think it's a good idea, include it in the meeting's agenda.

If your team meets up weekly to coordinate work, build in some non-work catching-up, too. By this, I don't mean prying into anyone's private life or pressuring them to share more than they want to. The idea is just to voluntarily talk about something beyond just work. This could be something tangential to work, such as an anecdote about a client. Let everyone be free to mention something personal if they want to. The best way to encourage others to open up is by doing it yourself and sharing something about you.

If you're all the same city, you could organize some informal face-to-face meetings to spend a couple of hours together. You could meet up to work or to do something else. A monthly meet-up outside work to do an activity that helps you get to know each other better will be team-building, which benefits you all.

27. Understand your inseparable colleague: you

Without a doubt, remote working is more solitary than work in an office. You're not surrounded by colleagues any more. You talk to them over the phone or by email, but that's not the same as having your colleague opposite you, that really funny one, firing off little jokes constantly. You miss it now.

After a day alone in your home office, with no one for company but your shadow and no one to talk to except via email, it's normal to feel alone. You'll feel desperate to see people, to meet friends, to spend time with family...anything to see another human being. That's natural, especially at the start. It's normal for people who work alone to feel that urgent need to socialize.

In time, you'll get used to this new way of working, without that joker of a colleague making your mornings go faster. You'll discover the many advantages of working in solitude: you can concentrate better because many interruptions are eliminated. Now that you're not hearing your colleague's jokes, you miss them, but don't you remember a time when the incessant one-liners were a pain in the butt?

While you're getting used to it, attend to your social needs. Any interaction with a human (or even a non-human, like a cat, dog or other pet) counts. Go out in the street, say "hi" to your neighbor, thank the cashier at the grocery store; these things may seem little, but any communication, no matter how small, helps to fulfil that need for social interaction. Phone a friend or relative. Meet up with someone for a mid-morning coffee. Make plans for after work. Go to networking sessions, and so on.

Little things can make you feel less alone. Simply working with music on works for some people. Listening to a podcast or radio show can help keep you company. Although they're not practices I generally recommend, since they divert your attention away from what you're doing, they can work well when the task you're working on is very repetitive, or when you're taking a break.

Every person needs a different level of day-to-day socialization. Extroverts need more contact with other people over the course of the day in order to feel good, while introverts are more tolerant of solitude. Here, by "extrovert" we mean someone who feels recharged after spending time with others, while introverts are people who recharge on their own. In either case, humans are social creatures, and we need to interact with others.

Understand yourself, and ask yourself: Do I feel alone? Ask yourself that question every day.

Some people who begin working remotely don't realize how lonely they feel until it's deeply internalized.

If, after all, remote working isn't for you, consider a coworking space. There, you'll be surrounded by people and feel that you're in the company of other workers. Some even organize social activities for their members, during and after the working day, which will help fulfil your need for socialization.

28. Have a weekly meeting with yourself

This is one of my favorite tips. I started holding meetings with myself a year and a half ago.

Even though I was well-organized with my tasks and my work for clients, I was finding it hard to fit my personal professional projects into my schedule.

One day, I realized that work teams hold weekly meetings to share what's happened over the course of the week and to organize themselves for the coming one.

I never get invited to that kind of meeting; I have no team, I work alone.

And it occurred to me: what if I met with myself to organize the week ahead? Would I find space for my abandoned projects? Since then, I've been meeting with myself every Monday morning (or, sometimes, on Sundays) and whenever I feel I need a meeting, I call one.

I'll tell you how I do it, just so you know – you can find your own method, of course.

I sit down with a cup of coffee; I often go to a café to hold this meeting. I start with just a little notebook. For the first part of the meeting, I think about everything I've done over the past week: what I've spent time on, what I didn't have time for, what got passed over, and so on. I note down ideas and check off completed tasks in my notebook. Then I think about the coming week: about what I want to do, what I have to do (note that these are two different things). I think beyond the end of the week, considering my long-term aims, too. Sometimes, new ideas come up – others, I throw out old ideas I've changed my mind about pursuing.

For the last part of the meeting, I get my computer and add to my schedule the tasks I'm going to do this week, assigning them a day and time.

I normally give myself an hour for that meeting. Sometimes I do it while traveling, or pick another place; but in general, I prefer to do it somewhere other than my normal workspace.

These meetings have enabled me to get an overall view of what I'm doing. Before, I would slot projects into my schedule as they arrived, which meant others never got done.

This idea of a weekly meeting may seem similar to organizing yourself simply by writing down any outstanding tasks and putting them into your schedule, but the results are different.

The weight and importance you give to a meeting is more than just sitting down with your schedule and a pen. A meeting is a formally planned event at a certain time and with a certain length. Sometimes, you even have to prepare before going to one.

Those intrinsic associations with the word "meeting" put you in a different headspace, and you take what you're doing more seriously.

I can promise you that they'll probably be the most productive meetings you've ever had. I can't promise there won't still be disagreements with the attendee, though ;)

29. Plan the day before

You get up in the morning and get to work. Eight hours later, you look back and realize you haven't done any of the things you really needed to do.

Has this ever happened to you? I'm sure it has. It's happened to all of us.

Starting work without a plan or clear objectives in mind is like sailing without a map. You may get somewhere, but it may not be the port you needed to go to, or you might just get lost on an immense sea.

You could spend the whole day working without having anything planned on your schedule. The hours often simply fill up without getting anything done that advances you toward your goals. Those are the days you spend putting out fires; going from task to task as they arise. Usually, this is because other people are sending you things to do. And if you do them, without even considering how important they really are, and whether they need to be done right now or if you have something more pressing waiting.

Those are the days when you start work without a plan. You were doing things, sure – but were you productive? Did you complete any tasks? Or did you just start a lot of them and not finish any? Did you reach that port by the end of your day? Was it the one you needed to sail to? I doubt it, because you didn't actually know where you wanted or needed to go. You may be satisfied with the destination you reached, in which case, you're lucky. By chance, you arrived at the right port. However, the likelihood of not liking the route you took or the place you got to by the end of the day is very high.

That's why it's important to make a plan based around your aims and what you need to do to achieve them. Setting sail without a map is risky; you won't get where you need to go, and you could get lost along the way. Nowadays, surrounded by distractions all around, drifting off course is all too easy.

Planning the day before is better than doing it the same morning. It allows you to look at the next day with a broader perspective and with more distance. We don't see the day the same way once we're already in it. When the day has already started, everything takes on a sense of urgency.

Just before you finish work for the day, you should do a sum-up of the day. Use this information to plan tomorrow; it will help you improve, replicate, or change things so you can organize your day.

When planning, always bear in mind your short-, medium- and long-term work objectives. This helps to give you a clearer image of what you need to prioritize, spend more time on, or push down your schedule.

This process shouldn't take you longer than five minutes, often less.

It will enable you to:

- End your working day without thoughts such as: "tomorrow I have to remember to…".
- Begin the process of switching off.
- Organize your day based more on what's important and less on what's urgent.
- Start the next day with a clear guide.

Another big advantage of planning the day before is that you can get straight to work without having to think about it. You'll avoid wondering *where do I start?* – a question that often leads to procrastination.

In any case, if you didn't plan out your day the day before, then do it first thing in the morning.

30. Celebrate what you've achieved

Look back over what you've done at the end of the day, week or month, and when finishing a project. Summing up what you've achieved and checking it off your to-do list is rewarding and motivating.

When you worked in the office, you had a more direct relationship with your colleagues, boss, clients, and so on. If you were lucky, they appreciated the work you did and occasionally showed you with a comment or a simple smile. When you work from home, many of these comments and subtle spontaneous displays of gratitude are lost.

When you don't have face-to-face contact with people, you don't see their body language – and some words that are more easily expressed in speech than in writing get lost, too. It's rarer that you celebrate anything. That on-a-whim drink you go for with colleagues on a Friday evening to celebrate making that big sale is less likely to happen.

If you're lucky enough to have a boss who appreciates and praises your work regularly, you'll notice that they express their approval less frequently now. You get less feedback when you are remote working.

That's why it's important to celebrate yourself – you have to be the one to acknowledge a job well done. Self-motivation is more important than ever now.

At the end of a given time period (a day, a week, a month, a quarter) look back at what you've accomplished. Use whatever method you prefer: check off tasks you've completed, write down all your little wins…Just stop for a moment and think about what you've done and what that means for your work and for you. Value the importance of the smallest achievements and how they contribute to something bigger.

Congratulate yourself. When you finish any task, even the tiny ones or the ones that have been stagnating on your to-do list for weeks, you deserve a little recognition for having completed it.

Give yourself a little pat on the back. Your boss isn't there to tell you how well you did, so you need to tell yourself.

31. Set an end to your working day

You can't possibly finish everything you need to do. Ever. It's impossible, because there's always something else to do. That's why it's not helpful to just keep extending your working day to infinity.

Set yourself working hours and time limits. If you don't your tasks will expand to fill all the time available. If you don't set a limit, those tasks will just keep stretching out endlessly in front of you. Setting a time for each task will help prevent work rolling on longer than it should.

Now that you're remote working, there's no going-home time. The temptation to keep working is always there – or should I say *here*. Work is nearby, right on your computer: usually close to you, to where you eat, where you watch TV, where you enjoying being with family.

Set a time to start and end your working day. When that time rolls around, stop working. If you lengthen the day a little today, tomorrow you'll give in to the same temptation, and the day after that, and after a few days you'll realize your working day is longer than you said it would be. If you decide to finish at five o'clock, but you keep on working till six, your body and mind will subconsciously get used to that extra hour of work. And without realizing it, you'll expand your tasks to fill that time. If you go back over what you've done, you'll realize that you spent more time working but you didn't get any more done. You don't do more – just the same amount, but in more time.

Of course, take this advice like the rest: with flexibility. It doesn't mean you can never work past 6pm, if that's the time you've decided on. If you have more work than usual one day, adjust that time. Try to do it before you start working. If you think work will take an hour longer than usual, tell yourself you'll "clock off" at 7pm.

32. Switch off

Once you've finished work for the day, switch off. Stop thinking about work. Why? Because your mind needs to.

Taking a break is necessary in order to stay productive. Respect your sleeping pattern, and the hours you dedicate to leisure, too.

Life outside work is important, you know that, and even if you're only concerned with your career then know that spending all day working with no time for yourself won't help you to grow professionally. If you don't sleep, do things for fun, or switch off, your energy and creativity will start to lag and your performance will suffer.

Forget about work and think about something else.

We talked about getting ready to start working in the morning and about creating some ritual that serves as a transition to help your mind get in work mode. When you leave the office, your journey home serves as a transition to stop thinking about work and start thinking about your home and personal life. That helps you to switch off.

If you find it hard to disconnect when you're working from home, create a switching-off ritual.

Planning the next day right before you finish work is a good way to end your day and tell your brain that's enough for today. If you need other rituals, here are a few ideas:

- Turn off your laptop and put it away.
- Put on special music that's different from the kind you listen to while you work.
- Go into a different room.
- Make yourself something to eat or drink.
- Go out for a walk.

Do that action consciously for several days in a row to help your brain associate it with the end of your working day.

33. Deal with inspiration properly when it comes

Switching off can sometimes have an unwanted side effect. Letting your mind go elsewhere can mean you suddenly get struck with new and creative ideas on something you'd been stuck on at work.

You could be watching a movie with your family and suddenly, like a bolt from the blue, a great idea hits you about that work matter you'd almost given up on. You get up off the couch – the movie wasn't that good anyway – and power up your laptop so you can take care of it then and there.

That's not a good or bad thing, but bear in mind it does come at a cost – to you and your family. You cut your leisure time short to go back to work. How is separating your work and personal life going for you? And more importantly, how does that affect you emotionally? Later, will you get the feeling you worked all week without even a weekend break? What about your family? How do they take it? And how do you feel about how it looks to your family that you leave them to go work when you're meant to be spending time with them?

Think about your answers to these questions. If you can't think of any reason not to go and get some work done, then do it. But if it's going to make you feel exhausted and as if you didn't rest all weekend just because you took a few hours to work, or if your family is going to be disappointed that you took off and that makes you feel bad, then maybe now isn't the best time to take care of that important matter. You have a more important personal matter to attend to, and right now it's time to do that.

Remote work sometimes means working when you don't feel like it, and not working when it's not time to.

If you've finished work and suddenly remember something you could have done or you have a brilliant idea, note it down on your phone or in a notebook and let it be until tomorrow.

If inspiration strikes you in the early hours of the morning, let it in. Welcome it, but take your hours of rest. And if you went to bed late because you were dealing with some helpful epiphany, try to get those hours of sleep back: get up later in the morning if you can, take a nap, or go to bed earlier the following night.

Those are all of our 33 tips for working remotely; I hope they're helpful to you and you can use them. Remember: the important thing is not what I've told you to do to make remote work more efficient. The important thing is for you to try, adapt and use only what works for you, your specific situation, and who you are.

If you still haven't downloaded your productivity journal, do it now (http://carmencorral.com/productivity-journal),

To help other people benefit from these 33 tips for working remotely, it would be great if you could leave a review of this book on Amazon. YOUR OPINION MATTERS, LEAVE A REVIEW HERE (bit.ly/workingremotely33).

If you have a question about remote work or a comment to make, don't hesitate to write to me at: carmen@carmencorral.com.

CARMEN CORRAL

33 more tips for developing your skills

Read it here: bit.ly/speaking33

Interesting further reading on productivity to apply to remote work:

- Timothy Ferriss, 2007, *The 4-Hour Work Week* (https://amzn.to/2ZqwKIv)

- David Heinemeier Hansson, Jason Fried, 2014, Remote: Office Not Required (https://amzn.to/2ERc6tZ)

- Greg Mckeown, 2014, *Essentialism: The Disciplined Pursuit of Less* (https://amzn.to/332Sue6)

- Michael Hyatt, 2019, Free to Focus: A Total Productivity System to Achieve More by Doing Less (https://amzn.to/2QUa2DT)

www.ingramcontent.com/pod-product-compliance
Lightning Source LLC
Chambersburg PA
CBHW031438210526
45464CB00005B/2254